Super Presti

West Riding 2

South Yorkshire and Bullocks

David W Allen

© 2005 David W Allen

ISBN 1 898432 40 6

Cover: **KWU 979** (**74**), a South Yorkshire 1951 all-Leyland PD2 is parked with **OWR 264** (**77**), a 1954 Leyland PD2 with bodywork by Bond, the first to have a 'tin front' and enclosed rear platform. *(David Allen Collection)*

Inside front cover: South Yorkshire, not prone to excessive publicity on the bus side of their business, did produce this timetable in 1962. Detail of their longest journey (Leeds - Pontefract - Doncaster) is itemised. *(SYRT)*

Inside rear cover: Bullocks produced their last timetable in 1949 as shown. A sample of their rack tickets is also shown. *(David Allen Collection)*

Rear cover: **AHL 926** (**294**) in the Bullock fleet was a 1947 AEC Regent III with Roe bodywork. It features in a rare colour print of a Bullock bus, taken during 1952 in Leeds, two years after West Riding took the company over. *(C Carter)*

Title page: A 1924 Lancia bus with a Bell of Finningley 20-seat body stands outside Bullocks premises in Cornmarket, Pontefract. These premises became the South Yorkshire Motors base in 1928. *(John Lambert Collection)*

Opposite page: Bullocks were one of the early users of the new all-Leyland double-deck bus, the Titan. *(John Banks Collection)*

Below: South Yorkshire Motors were loyal to the Albion *marque* until the end. Here we see a print of **AWY 948** (**46**), a 1935 Albion PW 67 model with English Electric coachwork. This was an Olympia Show model showing different registration plates.

SOUTH YORKSHIRE

THE MOTOR B & S SERVICE

Introduction and acknowledgements

West Riding 1 was published in early 2004, the year in which the West Riding Automobile Company would have celebrated its Centenary. It followed the company history from the tram era through to its loss of identity when finally absorbed by Arriva in 2000. This second volume now tracks the two major companies absorbed by West Riding, J Bullock and Sons (1928) Ltd (B & S Motor Services) of Featherstone in 1950 and then South Yorkshire Road Transport of Pontefract through Caldaire Holdings in 1994. Both those companies developed from the same Bullock family transport roots at the turn of the last century.

It is from these operators that my particular interest developed in the West Riding company. Living in Selby, a major base for Bullocks, I travelled extensively by their services in the postwar years of austerity in the 1940s and 1950s. First to Wakefield (via Leeds or Pontefract) before the direct service from Selby to Wakefield was reintroduced after the war. The relatives visited lived a few hundred yards from the two Bullock depots in Savile Street. Here, was seen the extensive body repair and overhaul work being carried out on this varied, overworked fleet after the second world war. Later I travelled daily to school in York by B & S sampling the prewar Leyland TD and utility fleet of Daimler COG5 and CWA6 double-deckers often "put out to grass" on the flat routes around Selby.

This was followed by joining the industry with West Yorkshire Road Car Ltd, eventually working at most of the depots in their wide geographical area including the Harrogate head office. It was from here on a memorable staff excursion to the 1958 Rugby Cup Final during the London bus strike that I met my future wife. But that is another story. After National Service with the RAF Air Traffic Control in the Middle East, a return was made to the bus industry for a few years. After a period with South Yorkshire Motors Ltd, I moved to another part of the transport industry, but always kept an interest in the bus sector.

I would like to express my appreciation in particular to John Bennett, John Lambert and John McCloy for their help and access to comprehensive records of the Bullock and South Yorkshire fleet and family, and once again to The PSV Circle and The Omnibus Society for their fleet records. Thanks are also due to the various photographers known and unknown whose work illustrates this book, not forgetting John Banks and the Venture staff once again for their continued support and enthusiasm.

David W Allen FCILT
Whitkirk, Leeds
January 2005

South Yorkshire Road Transport Ltd

South Yorkshire Motors, or South Yorkshire Road Transport as it was known in the last years of operation, provided a small but efficient network of services centred on its base in Pontefract. The dark- and light-blue livery applied to the buses gave a distinctive and smart appearance. South Yorkshire remained in the original Bullock family ownership from 1929 until 1994 when it sold out to the Caldaire Group passing into the control of the West Riding Automobile Company - itself a large subsidiary of the Caldaire Group. This Group in 1998 passed to British Bus and then Cowie Holdings, which became Arriva PLC shortly afterwards. South Yorkshire's Pontefract base became Arriva Yorkshire (South) Ltd and its services were fully integrated into the existing West Riding operation. The attractive South Yorkshire two-tone blue livery finally disappeared in 2000.

1925 - The Winder Family

The company origins go back to the Winder family of Thorpe Audlin, Pontefract. May (the mother) and Raymond William Cuthbert (the son) commenced trading as the Badsworth Motor Company in 1925 with a bus and car given by her father. In 1926 the company was renamed South Yorkshire Motor Company, taking in Joan, the daughter. Licences were granted and a service started from Badsworth to Pontefract, followed by others from Pontefract to Doncaster via Askern and Pontefract to Doncaster via Barnsdale Bar. The Leeds to Doncaster direct service finally started in spring 1927. In September 1926 a Leeds, Pontefract, Doncaster to London service commenced - the first long distance express bus service licensed from Leeds to operate daily. This was quite a feat for a small company relying on the road conditions of the day with minimum logistical support. About the same time the London express service was advertised to be extended to and from Bradford, but whether this reached fruition at that time is uncertain. An unsuccessful application was also made for a Leeds to Sheffield express service.

At this time, both West Riding and Barnsley and District had become interested in South Yorkshire and an approach was made in 1927, but the asking price of £30,000 was not acceptable. Edmund Alfred Winder also commenced trading with Leyland PLSC buses from a Hemsworth address as Hallamshire Transport Company in late 1928, possibly in connection with the proposed Leeds to Sheffield express service. By this time the South Yorkshire Motor company was running into financial difficulties, not helped by their booking agent in Leeds, Wilkes Garage in Templar Street, operating in competition on the London service. In August 1929, the company was placed into liquidation showing a deficit of £10,000 with assets of only £54.

1929 - The Bullock Involvement

It was at this time that Ernest P Bullock arrived on the scene and purchased both Winder companies in August 1929 after leaving B & S Motor Services. The South Yorkshire business included the Leeds/Pontefract to Doncaster services as well as the daily Bradford/Leeds to London express. In January 1933, London, Midland and Yorkshire Services Ltd was formed incorporating B&E Ltd (E J Heath and G H Ennifer) of Doncaster and South Yorkshire (who also bought out the London service of Wilkes Parlour Car Services of Leeds at this time) to co-ordinate their London services. Three services a day were being operated to the city. Ernest Bullock was a director of this new company, but it had a short life, selling out to West Yorkshire Road Car Co Ltd, who purchased the company on behalf of the newly formed group of express service operators trading as Yorkshire Services in November 1934. The formation and history of the Yorkshire Services Pool is documented in the Yorkshire Coaching Pools Prestige Series book by Keith Healey.

A variety of buses came with the Winder businesses including Reos, Chevrolets, Leyland PLSC3s and Dennis E and F models. The Dennis buses had Ramsden of Liversedge 32-seat bus bodies. Three Studebaker Big Six 20-seat vehicles used on the London express service were also involved. Most of these vehicles were described as 'not being in good condition' when taken over. E P Bullock was one of the earliest users of the diesel engine with the first ones being used in 1931. In late 1933 he converted one of Winder's Leyland PLSCs to diesel power with a Gardner 4LW engine at a cost of £430. So successful was this that a further eight of the Albion buses he had recently purchased were converted at a cost of £395 each in 1934. After twelve months the total conversion costs had been recovered, such was the fuel cost differential at that time.

The company was renamed South Yorkshire Motors Ltd in 1930. E P Bullock and his son J R (Reg) Bullock operated the company from Ernest Bullock's own premises, which had been used by B & S Motor Services, in Cornmarket, Pontefract. The premises were enlarged to incorporate a retail garage and bus depot. This was to remain the company base until 1973.

Other stage carriage services were soon started: Pontefract to Hemsworth and Barnsley (taken over from Messrs Weavers Blue Bus Service of Brierley, operated jointly with Yorkshire Traction); Whitley Bridge and Selby, with a service to Doncaster via Womersley and Askern; and some colliery contract services. A summer only express service was operated to Bridlington from Pontefract with connections to Doncaster, Barnsley and Normanton, but this was discontinued in 1940 and was never restarted after the war.

During this period the major part of the company developed vehicle distribution and garage servicing from an early mixed-franchise business including Morris cars to major Ford Main Dealerships in Pontefract and later in Wakefield and Castleford. A tractor/agriculture business was also developed in Pontefract and Wakefield. The Ford dealerships continued as the major part of the total business into the 1970s.

Ernest Bullock's early enthusiasm for Albion Motors' products soon manifested itself with an order for six Viking PMA 28 models, the first being WX 1533 (30) with a Plaxton 32-seat body. They all came into service during early 1930. Most were rebodied during their lifetime and some given new fleet numbers. WX 2326 (35), for example, received a Burlingham utility body, giving 20 years' service. In the late 1930s a number were rebuilt

in South Yorkshire's own body shop, some to an English Electric design, and all were finally withdrawn in the late 1940s.

A further two Reo 24 seat Speed Wagons WX 1761 (31) and WX 2158 (32) were also purchased in 1929, probably to replace the costly Studebakers used on the London service.

Further Albion PW67/69 Valkyrie single-deck buses came on stream during the 1930s mostly with the Ribble Motors-inspired English Electric 31-seat coach bodies. These coaches were used on the stage carriage services and gave an exceptional standard of comfort that was to be continued when the double-deck fleet was established in the 1940s.

1940   The Double-Deck Era

As the second world war broke out, plans were made to replace four Albion Viking and Leyland PLSC buses with Daimler COG5/40s fitted with Burlingham single-deck bodies. However, these orders were subsequently changed by the Ministry of Supply to one for Daimler CWA6 utility double-deckers. The last bus produced to prewar standards arrived in 1941 - an Albion Valkyrie CX13 with Duple 35-seat bodywork, DYG 53 (51). The Duple body was of a type not dissimilar to a design which the Red and White Group of South Wales was taking at that time. DYG 53 had the all-new Albion 9.08-litre engine and was renowned as a speedy machine. It received a Burlingham coach body from Albion Valiant JWT 112 (57) in 1958.

At the commencement of the second world war in 1939, the curtailment of evening services and an immediate 50% reduction of service frequency during the day put heavy pressure on the single-deck fleet. These restrictions, however, were slightly relaxed within the year. The first of four lowbridge utility double-deck buses arrived in 1943: a Duple-bodied Daimler CWA6 55 seater followed by three more Daimlers with Duple or Brush bodies (52-5); all four were equipped with the standard utility slatted wooden seating. They were all eventually refurbished and equipped with high-backed seating. These were the first double-deck buses in the fleet.

Nineteen-forty-six saw the purchase of three Albion Valkyrie CX13s with austere Pickering

The "VICTOR" 20 SEATER

is made to fit country roads

THE Albion "VICTOR" is in its element on narrow country roads because its overall width is only 6 ft. 2 ins. It has all the features of a large bus, but everything is on a smaller scale—including running costs.

We shall be pleased to demonstrate to you at your place of business, if you will inform us of a convenient date.

It's an Albion

34-seat bodies (58-60), followed by a similar chassis carrying a Burlingham 33-seat coach body (61), and a Venturer CX19 with Strachan 55-seat double-deck bodywork (56) in 1947. The Albion era was now coming to a close, with the last models coming in 1950, including three Venturer CX37 Strachan double-deckers (70-2).

Albion Valiant JWT 112 (57) had the unusual distinction of being rebuilt and rebodied by Roe in 1958 as a double-decker and reregistered TWY 8 (81) with its original Burlingham body going to 1942 Valkyrie DYG 53 (now 57). Number 57 then spent five years as works transport and was preserved in 1969.

In 1951 a long association with Leyland commenced with the arrival of four all-Leyland PD2/12s (73-6). They had the appealing Leyland-designed bodywork and were equipped to the usual interior high standard of all South Yorkshire buses. By 1955, when the next two double-deckers were placed in service, rear doors and concealed radiators had become standard features.To supplement the high standard of Dunlopillo foam seating already used, Formica-type interior panelling was introduced at this time, eliminating the need for interior painting. Fluorescent lighting was also incorporated. The two Leyland PD2/20 s (77/8) concerned had rare Bond bodies - a little-known Lancashire coachbuilder - followed two years later in 1957 by a further two Leyland PD2/20 Park Royal double-deckers (79/80).

The last half cab buses came in 1960. They were Nos 82/3, two Leyland PD3/1s bodied by Roe as 30ft-long buses, giving a seating capacity of 63 against the previous standard of 55. The additional length gave them a sleek appearance. Few bodies of this length and type were being built at that time, the orthodox lowbridge layout with the sunken gangway upstairs by then being somewhat old fashioned.

Following the loan of a Yorkshire Traction Leyland Atlantean, this rear-engined chassis made its first appearance in the fleet in 1963 as two PDR1/1s (84/5) with 70-seat lowbridge Weymann bodies, again with fittings and furnishings above average and with extra legroom in line with South Yorkshire policy.

The pattern and style of service buses was now set for the next twenty years with the early Leyland Atlanteans bodied by Weymann followed by Leyland-powered Daimler Fleetlines and finally Leyland Olympians, all with Northern Counties bodies. Throughout its 40 years of operation South Yorkshire's fleet size did not exceed 20 until the last few years of expansion.

In 1968 South Yorkshire lost its long-serving Managing Director, Reg Bullock, and a period of change began to evolve as John M McCloy, a grandson of E P Bullock, took over. E P Bullock, the founder of the company, had died in 1962. The Ford dealership and garage business in Wakefield, Castleford and Pontefract were sold during the early 1970s, and the tractor/agricultural side closed down.

1973 South Yorkshire Road Transport Ltd

South Yorkshire Road Transport Ltd under John McCloy with David, his brother, as co-director, was reformed on 25th June 1973 to continue the bus business. The company was renamed because of the voluntary liquidation status of the former company. The traditional base was moved from Cornmarket to converted premises in Northgate, Pontefract. The reformed company made some changes to the conservative lines on which the previous operations had depended, particularly with the development of a dedicated coach fleet.

The Bellgraphic ticket machines, which had been in use for many years, were withdrawn and replaced with the Ultimate type. Earlier still Bell Punch and Willebrew had also been used. By June 1976, the modern Almex ticket issuing system had been brought into use. The first Daimler Fleetline/Northern Counties double-deckers (92-4) were introduced in August 1973, replacing three of the first all-Leyland PD2s, which had given 20 years' service. The new Fleetlines sported a striking revised livery using the same basic colours with white replacing the traditional cream lining in blocks rather than broad bands, with bold white lettering.

There had been little change to the route pattern over the previous 40 years. A limited stop service, however, was now introduced between Pontefract (Cobblers Lane Estate) and Leeds, branded as 'Timesaver'. A more innovative operation was planned in the form of an express service between Hull and Manchester, which finally commenced in September 1975, not without difficulty. The National Bus Company lodged objections to the original proposal and the outcome was two separate services: Castleford to Hull via Pontefract and M62, and Pontefract to Manchester via Castleford and M62. The service was withdrawn in January 1980.

This period introduced a change in fleet types with more emphasis being given to coach operations including private hire. Many coaches were obtained over the next twenty years both new and used, along with the standard Daimler Fleetlines, followed by Leyland Olympians for the stage carriage services. The first coach purchased for many years came in November 1973, Volvo B58/Duple Dominant 53 seater OWT 1M (1) and then SWU 2 M (2) in 1974. These were followed by two Leyland Leopard/Duple Dominant coaches (3/4). Further Volvo and Leyland Leopard coaches arrived during 1975.

An unusual arrival was two AEC Reliance/Marshall buses (8/9) ex-Yorkshire Woollen, the first of a number of second-hand purchases, although other such vehicles were coaches, mainly of Volvo and Leyland manufacture. Fleet numbers of these vehicle types usually related to the registration digits.

During 1975 the total operated annual mileage of the company had reached one million for the first time, the increased private hire and express services bringing this about.

In 1976 two more coaches (ex-Barton) entered the fleet: AEC Reliances with Plaxton coachwork (10/1). This brought the total fleet size to 24, ten being single-deck, mostly coaches. However, the two ex-Barton coaches had a short life and were replaced in 1977 by two Leyland Leopard/Plaxton coaches: UUM 77R (7) with 53 seat Supreme coachwork; and VWY 614S (14) with 45-seat Viewmaster coachwork. Both were equipped with tables and No. 14 was appropriately named 'Queen Elizabeth II' at the time of Her Majesty's Silver Jubilee. During this period there was some South Yorkshire interest in bus and coach rallies, the company securing awards in the 1977 British Coach Rally.

In 1978 an extension to the existing garage and workshop in Northgate was completed and in 1979 the company celebrated its Golden Jubilee. The first Leyland Olympians supplied to a private company joined the fleet in 1982 with the familiar bodies provided by Northern Counties (101/2). Further Leyland Royal Tiger coaches also arrived.

In October 1985, South Yorkshire acquired the established coach and bus business of Fords of Ackworth. No vehicles were involved, but five local services came with the business - mostly contract colliery operations.

In October 1986 the Selby service was withdrawn. It had been a weekend and Monday market day only service for many years. All journeys now terminated at Whitley Bridge. Two return journeys, Monday to Friday through to Selby, were reinstated in April 1993.

With the formation of the West Yorkshire Passenger Transport Authority, certain route numbers were allocated to services within the authority's area. Destination blinds showed the new numbers, the major Leeds to Doncaster service for example being 410. In 1987 some evening services were also taken over from West Riding between Doncaster and Knottingley under tender from the WYPTE. The Company was able to secure grants from both WYPTE and SYPTE in this period.

South Yorkshire had managed to provide the luxury of crew-operated buses into the latter part of 1987, when one-man-operation was eventually introduced. Reduction of local authority subsidies, colliery closures and ensuing economic problems led to some reduction in traffic in the area, and consequently revenue.

In July 1994 South Yorkshire sold out to the Caldaire Group. The coaching side of the business was disbanded and the coaches sold. The last new buses South Yorkshire purchased were three Dennis Dart/Plaxton Pointers (51-3). As these were non-standard vehicles in the Caldaire fleet, they were sold to Yorkshire Traction and replaced with Optare Metroriders.

South Yorkshire remained an autonomous unit operating from its original base in Pontefract. The blue company colour scheme was adapted to follow the Caldaire and then British Bus house style. Operating closely with its sister company, West Riding, inevitably there was an exchange of vehicles. Sadly, within four years both South Yorkshire and

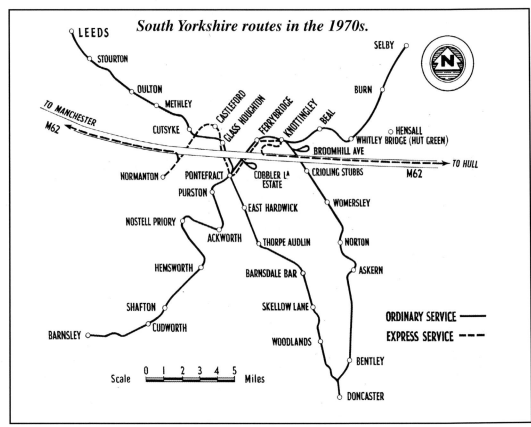

South Yorkshire routes in the 1970s.

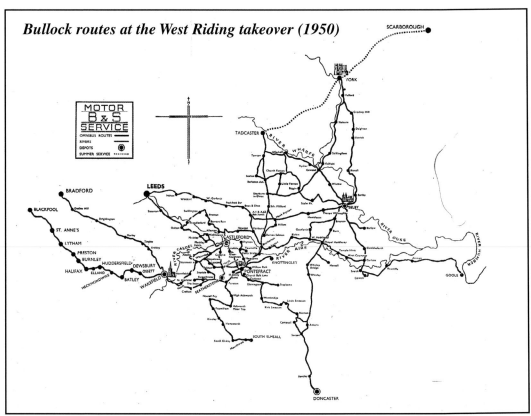

Bullock routes at the West Riding takeover (1950)

West Riding lost their identity as further consolidation took place in the industry and Arriva became involved. What was left of the original Bullock enterprise, established so long before, had now gone forever.

However, there are at least three preserved South Yorkshire buses: rebodied 1942 Albion Valkyrie/Burlingham coach DYG 53 (57); 1947 Albion Valkyrie/Duple GWT 630 (61); and the 1950 Albion Valiant rebuilt with Roe double-deck body TWY 8 (81), which is the only known Albion Valiant chassis with a double-deck body.

Finally, South Yorkshire's last hidden moment of fame may be the victory parade of the 2003 England Rugby League Team in London. It took place in an open top Leyland Olympian alleged to be former TWY 7, once registered to the company. In the same year the Northgate premises in Pontefract were demolished.

J Bullock & Sons (1928) Ltd (B & S Motor Services)

J Bullock and Sons (1928) Ltd, of Featherstone, trading as B & S Motor Services, was absorbed by the West Riding Automobile Company Ltd in September 1950. It was the largest acquisition made by West Riding. They had been rivals for over 30 years and were two of the largest independent bus companies of their day in the country. Bullocks had 170 vehicles and the new combined fleet doubled the size of West Riding overnight to some 400 buses. Their colourful fleet of maroon, crimson and cream vehicles was built up by Bullocks with orders for buses from numerous chassis and body builders. To say the least, the variety of the Bullock fleet in its final years was a bus enthusiast's dream. Throughout the company's existence vehicles were obtained from no fewer than 26 chassis manufacturers and 22 coachbuilders - and all new except those from acquired companies. Bullock's final operating area covered a large part of the old West Riding including York, Selby, Goole and Doncaster in the East through to Pontefract, Castleford, Wakefield, Leeds and Bradford in the West. Its main operating depots were in Featherstone and Wakefield with satellite bases at Selby and Doncaster. As well as private hire work, a regular all year round express service was operated from Wakefield to Blackpool. Regular summer express services and excursions to both east and west coasts were operated from all depot locations and surrounding areas.

The Early Years

James Bullock established a mixed greengrocery business in Station Lane, Featherstone, well before the end of the 19th century. As his six sons grew up, the family interests expanded into transport and catering. The transport side covered horse-drawn wagons, wagonettes, charabancs, removal vans and funeral carriages. One of their early contracts was the supply of horses to the Featherstone fire brigade. As early as 1900 a formal business agreement was set up among all the brothers. The first recorded motor vehicle appeared in 1909 in the form of a chain-driven Karrier charabanc with a toastrack body. It was driven in those early days by James (Jim) Bullock Jnr, who had been taught to drive by Karrier in Huddersfield. He was to become an important figure in the development of the company. By November 1911, Bullocks were advertising in the local paper a motor landaulet for hire which appeared to be a form of taxi of French origin.

J Bullock and Sons Ltd was the registered company set up on the 5th June 1913 "to carry on business as omnibus and motor coach proprietors" as well as furniture removers, fish-dealer and fruiterer with E P Bullock as the Managing Director. The first regular daily public motor service commenced in November 1914, operating an hourly service between Pontefract and Featherstone six days a week. During the difficult period of the first world war, Bullocks, like many other fledgling operators, had most of their motorised vehicles requisitioned. One or two vehicles were retained and allocated for the transport of essential war workers to the ordnance factory in Crossgates, Leeds, and a similar facility at Horbury, Wakefield. The rest of the business had to rely on the horses. But in 1916 Bullocks were allocated a Daimler 29-seat charabanc (C 5545) to assist in the transport of essential war workers. This eventually became fleet

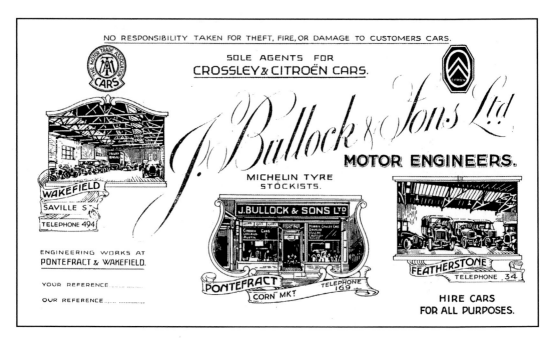

number 2 and the first to be registered as a public service vehicle, in 1921, as required by the 1920 Road Traffic Act. Various vehicle types were purchased after the war. The year 1919 saw three Daimler CKs, two Leylands and a Maudslay arrive, some of which had alternative bodies for goods work.

1920s - and Growing Pains

This decade proved to be a significant period in the Bullocks' history. Regular services were being operated between Leeds, Normanton, Castleford, Pontefract and surrounding districts. Regular market-day services to such places as Selby and Dewsbury, and excursions to race meetings and east and west coastal resorts were a growing business. A host of vehicles from different manufacturers were purchased and inherited, including Daimler CKAs, Leyland Z5, GH7, A13, C7 models, Albion PF24, PK26 Lancia, Gotfredson and AEC 411; many had Strachan and Brown bodies. Towards the end of the 1920s as vehicle types developed some standardisation appeared, with Albions and Leyland PLSC Lions carrying locally built bodies by such as Bell of Finningley, Clark of Scunthorpe and Harrison of Dewsbury, arriving on the scene. By this time the company had become known and traded as B & S Motor Services.

During the mid twenties the roles of the various brothers became clearer. Dennis Bullock, the eldest brother, concentrated on the removals side of the business establishing separate premises in Featherstone. Abraham (Abe) managed premises in Cornmarket, Pontefract, which provided general garage and repair facilities with an early Morris car franchise. Coach bookings were also taken. These premises eventually became the South Yorkshire Motors operating base. Abraham was to be come a significant figure as the bus business developed.

John and "Wally" Bullock took jobs at the main Featherstone depot in Wilson Street. Ernest Bullock, the second eldest brother, and the nominal head of the business, was in charge at Featherstone. He had a strong preference for Albion vehicles. Jim Bullock, who assisted Ernest, developed the Wakefield end of the business and an operating base was established. Spare land off Savile Street in Wakefield provided the first base, initially for early morning colliery transport. Temporary accommodation was erected and the same buses were used to operate the new local services to Featherstone, Pontefract, Normanton and Castleford. Eventually this part of Wakefield was to become a major operating base for the company with two established depots. Jim appeared to work with some autonomy and Leyland vehicles were purchased for the Wakefield operations. By the late 1920s, the company had well over 50 vehicles. Leylands and Albions continued to be the core of vehicle purchases. Four major operators had been or were being taken over: Healds of Normanton, Smiths of Selby, Masson of Hemsworth and Bennett of Askern. Others included Lowe of Altofts, Rowley of Hemsworth, Millman and Dresser of Fairburn, and Stockwell of Woodlesford. The B & S operating area had more or less reached its maturity, with established depots in Featherstone, Wakefield (1920), Selby (1928), Normanton and Askern (1929) - later transferred to Doncaster. In 1923 the Featherstone operation was moved from Station Road to a yard off Wilson Street where the headquarters and major operating base was established.

During this period the speed at which Bullocks were developing their bus business in the Pontefract/Castleford/Wakefield district did not go unnoticed. This was the heartland of the Yorkshire (West Riding) Electric Tramway Company operating area. West Riding had been operating trams in this part of Yorkshire since the beginning of the century. Now faced with falling passenger traffic with the advent of the motor bus, and also track maintenance problems, it took remedial action which had first been actively considered before the outbreak of war in 1914.

In 1922 the tramway company ordered their first 22 Bristol buses. This was quickly followed by further orders and the West Riding Automobile Company was officially set up as the operating company in 1923. During a period of only 3 years to 1926, Bullock's main competitor had built up a fleet of buses in excess of 100. Negotiations commenced between the two companies about a possible merger. A draft agreement was even prepared. But Bullocks withdrew at a late hour. In fact they had their own internal management problems, which were to become apparent within a short period. This was a major factor in the breakdown of negotiations with West Riding at that time.

General competition during the post war period had been considerable. Road 'piracy' had become a common feature of early bus operations, with speed being a major factor. For this purpose Bullocks purchased some Italian SPAs and Lancias together with Gotfredsons - speedy machines in their day - to compete with the new buses West Riding, in particular, were purchasing. This was important on the prestigious routes such as Leeds and Wakefield to Castleford and Pontefract. Not being designed for stage-carriage-type work, these buses did not prove as reliable as the new breed of vehicles coming on stream from Leyland, Albion, Bristol and other British manufacturers. But Bullocks still had some edge at this time, being ahead of the competition in having pneumatic tyres fitted to their vehicles.

However, 1928 proved to be a watershed year in the company's history. As already mentioned, there had been friction for some time on how the business should be managed between E P (Ernest) Bullock, the nominal head of the business, and his brothers. Not only had this led to a stalemate in the prolonged negotiations with the West Riding company, more importantly this disagreement led to an expensive High Court action. At the Court of Appeal, Lord Justice Scrutton giving judgement said, among other comments:

'Ernest was a strong man. One of his younger brothers (Jim) was also a strong man. They were all Yorkshiremen: when two strong Yorkshiremen worked together it was usually probable that a time would come when the irresistible force met the immovable post - and indeed it did'.

Ernest Bullock left and acquired the ailing South Yorkshire Motor Company of Thorpe Audlin, Pontefract, including the associated Hallamshire Transport Company of Hemsworth. He took with him his strong allegiance to the Albion brand of vehicles, and retained his own extensive property in Cornmarket, Pontefract (which Bullocks had been renting), for his new company.

The reconstituted public company (J Bullock and Sons (1928) Ltd) was registered as such on the 3rd January 1929 and was headed by Jim Bullock as Managing Director and Abraham (Abe) Bullock as Company Secretary. The trading name of B & S Motor Services was retained and the registered offices remained in Featherstone. A period of

From every point of view...

STRACHANS

SUCCESSORS LTD

CONTRACTORS TO H.M. GOVERNMENT

LEAD THE WAY

Distinguished design, superb comfort and smoothly balanced streamlining contribute to the supremacy of Strachan's coachwork. Many years of unique practical experience, and superb craftsmanship give Strachans the leadership in coachbuilding which is maintained in an impressive display of technique and workmanship to meet every need of modern passenger road transport services.

consolidation and further growth now seemed assured with a fleet of buses which had grown to nearly 100.

1930s - Pattern for the Future

Most competition had now been eliminated. The Government of the day was concerned that public safety was being put at risk with under-financed buses chasing each other for business, particularly by operators failing to meet a satisfactory maintenance standard. The same operators often ran to no fixed timetables.

To further complicate operations, various local authorities through which the buses ran had their own bye-laws regarding these 'hackney carriages', with local Watch Committees granting licences. In Leeds, for example, passengers were not allowed to smoke or stand on buses operating within the city boundary. Hence the 1930 Road Traffic Act which brought about regulations and licensing of all bus services bringing some order to the industry. Both Bullocks and West Riding had come to an 'understanding' of these problems well before the Act came into force, and had taken appropriate action, especially with well-timetabled journeys. Bullocks were, in fact, the last independent company to receive a licence from the Leeds Watch Committee - in September 1930 for a miners' special from Leeds to Woodlesford - before the Road Traffic Act came into force.

Nineteen-thirty saw the purchase of 17 new buses: Leyland LT1s and LT2s, AEC Regals, Daimler CF6s, an Albion PKA 26 and a Dennis G type. Most of the Leylands had Leyland bodies. The Daimlers (112/3) were particularly smart coaches, bodied by Taylors of Barnsley, with sliding roofs, curtains and luggage racks but they saw only six years' service. By this time Bullocks had a range of services radiating from Leeds to Goole via Selby, Knottingley via Castleford, Doncaster via Pontefract, and other services to Hemsworth and South Elmsall. Most used Sovereign Street as the terminus. Leeds to Goole and York to Doncaster were the two longest routes in the network, and were operated by Selby and Doncaster depots. In geographical terms, the expansion of Bullocks services was quicker and larger than that of West Riding during this period.

Quite a variety of vehicle types came into the fleet in the 1930s. The first double-deckers appeared in 1931: three lowbridge Leyland TD1s (118-20). All future double-deck buses would be of the lowbridge type. These petrol engine buses received Gardner 5LW or 6LW units during their early life. At the same time, further Leyland LT2s and LT3s arrived which appeared to have Taylor of Barnsley bodies. A rather odd acquisition at the time was No. 127, a Commer Invader 20-seater which lasted only four years. The following year saw the arrival of four AEC Regals (134-7) with Barnsley Motor bodies. (This company appears to have merged with Taylors of Barnsley.) These buses gave good service: three of them lasted into the West Riding days; all were rebodied.

At this time B & S began a programme of rebuilding several of the 1926/7 Albion PK26s, giving them a new lease of life. In 1932 a further two all Leyland TD2s arrived (143/4) along with two Leyland KP3 Cubs (141/2). Titan No. 144 had a particularly long life, being rebuilt in 1949 and spending its last years at Selby depot into the West Riding era. In 1934 two Weymann-bodied AEC Q types were purchased (161/2), one diesel, one petrol, principally for private-hire work. The AEC Q type was a landmark in bus development in many ways. It had an engine mounted to the offside with an entrance forward of the front axle: a design influenced to some extent by American practice. Both these futuristic vehicles, based at Featherstone, gave a certain amount of trouble and had relatively short lives. More Leyland LT5As and some Daimler CP6s arrived, the latter with smart Roberts of Horbury coach bodies (168/9).

Another CP6 coach (185) arrived in 1936 with a Brush 32-seat body. It had been a Commercial Show exhibit. Two Willowbrook-bodied Daimler COG5 double-deckers also came on the scene, one with an unusual front entrance and two aisles on the top deck (170). Barnaby of Hull rebuilt these buses with conventional bodies in 1944/5. At this time B & S were operating a service very much out on a limb from Pontefract to Tadcaster and York, and through York to Haxby. By all accounts a lot of empty mileage was run and traffic receipts were poor. Meanwhile the West Yorkshire Road Car Company had taken over

York city services and Corcoran - a Tadcaster based operator. Naturally West Yorkshire was keen to take over these Bullock routes. A deal was done and an exchange was made with Corcoran's Tadcaster to Pontefract service.

By the mid thirties the early generation buses obtained in the late twenties, which included many absorbed during take-overs, began to be withdrawn. These included Dennis Gs, Leyland PLSCs, Albion PM28s, and the last Gotfredson. An assortment of new buses and coaches continued to be purchased from a variety of chassis and bodybuilders. AEC and Leyland provided the bulk of the chassis, with Barnaby of Hull becoming the favoured supplier of single-deck bodies in bus and coach form. AEC Regals Nos 197/8 carried the first Barnaby bodies.

Bullocks themselves had an active bodyshop, first in Featherstone and later in Savile Street, Wakefield, which had been their first purpose-built garage in Wakefield. An attractive coachbuilt body was designed and constructed by them on a Daimler CP6 chassis (195) with distinctive Brush type features in 1936 and was the pride of the fleet for many years. It was the last of that chassis type produced. A second larger garage was completed at this time, also in Savile Street, and survived as such until the late 1990s. The same period saw considerable investment in further purpose-built premises at all their locations in Selby, Featherstone and Doncaster. In 1937 Roe became a supplier of double-deck bodies with the first order on two AEC Regents (216/7), which spent much of their early life at the small Doncaster depot working along the A19 to Selby and York. Leyland also supplied bodies for double-deckers.

The single-deckers during this period were mostly Willowbrook-bodied Daimler COG5s. One of these buses, BWW 475 (202), was in fact another 1936 Commercial Show model. This purchasing pattern continued into 1940 before wartime manufacturing restrictions came into force.

At least six buses were quickly earmarked for wartime activity. A Leyland TS7 (196) was converted to an ambulance and stationed at Featherstone; an AEC Regal (135) was converted to a mobile theatre for troop entertainment; and AEC Regent 149 went down to London on loan for a short period in 1940 (based at Chiswick). Other vehicles were requisitioned by Northern Command, York.

1940s - The Final Decade

As wartime restrictions gradually came into force, timetables were adjusted to reduce mileage. Women were employed as conductors and drivers for the first time as staff shortages began to be felt. Evening journeys took the largest cutback. Some of the longer through routes such as Wakefield to Selby, were withdrawn completely. A few of the older buses, especially the TD1s and TD2s, were fitted with producer-gas trailers and used on the major flat routes, particularly into Leeds from Castleford/Pontefract. The first new vehicles allocated under austerity conditions ('utilities') came in 1942: three were Bedford OWBs and there were two Guy Arab 1s with Roe bodies. The Bedfords were used in the Selby area particularly for the rural routes using the Cawood river bridge with its weight restriction. By 1943 a further two Bedford/Duples had been added to the fleet along with 2 Daimler CWG5 double-deckers with Brush bodies. A further pair of Guy Arab 1s, one each with NCME and Roe bodywork, also arrived. These Arabs fitted with the Gardner 5LW engine were heavy and proved very sluggish.

Through 1944 and 1945 more Daimler CWA/CWD 6s arrived with Duple or Brush bodies, mostly with relaxed utility bodywork. All the Bedford OWBs had slatted wooden seats for most of their life; the other utility double-deckers had a variety of upholstered seating, including lightly covered slatted seats. At least one Daimler CWA6, AHL 66 (267), operated with wooden slatted seats into the West Riding era. Barnaby as well as Cawoods of Doncaster, along with other small coachbuilders, continued to rebody or refurbish buses during and after the war years, supplementing the Bullock Savile Street repair shop facilities.

Daimlers continued to be strong favourites in single- and double-deck form as peacetime conditions slowly returned, no doubt because of wartime production continuation. Strachan bodies on some of the early postwar Daimler double-deckers had to be extensively rebuilt in

J. BULLOCK & SONS (1928) LTD.

DEPÔTS AT
WAKEFIELD 'PHONE 2494.
CASTLEFORD " 142.
PONTEFRACT " 169.
SELBY " 263.

MOTOR
B&S
SERVICE

ALL COMMUNICATIONS
TO BE ADDRESSED TO:-
HEAD OFFICE
FEATHERSTONE.
—— PHONE 30. ——

Registered Office:-
WILSON STREET,
FEATHERSTONE.

West Riding days; others were prematurely withdrawn because of structural problems. However, Leylands began to reappear in 1947 in the form of PS1s with single-deck Barnaby or Willowbrook dual-purpose coachwork and, of course, the double-deck all-Leyland PD2s. Most of the PS1s received Roe double-deck bodies in early West Riding days giving them a long service life.

Services were increased again as new vehicles began to arrive and the backlog of maintenance interrupted during the war was reduced. Between 1948 and 1950 an assortment of vehicles was purchased including AEC Regents and Regals, Leyland PS/PDs, Seddon Mk 4s, Guy Arab IIIs, bodied by an equal assortment of coachbuilders including yet another new one, Longford of Neath, who provided the last luxury coachwork for Bullocks on two Leyland PS2s (339/40). This coachbuilder also rebodied a prewar Leyland TD5 and a number of Leyland TSs with luxury bodies about the same time.

1950 - The End

By 1950, nearly three quarters of the country's stage carriage services were in the hands of large groups like Tilling, Scottish Motor Group or BET, or were municipally owned. The fear of regional nationalisation similar to that of the road haulage industry was real. Wage costs were increasing, and so was private motoring. Abraham Bullock expressed these fears at the

time. A projected merger with West Riding seemed a prudent measure to reduce duplication by some pruning and avoid an increase in fares. An "amalgamation" of the two companies finally took effect in September 1950 with West Riding paying in the region of £500,000 for the Bullock company with 170 vehicles. It was outwardly a smooth transition, with the small Doncaster depot of Bullocks being the only major casualty. Both Jim and Abraham Bullock maintained a position in the enlarged company. West Riding was now the largest independent bus company in the country, and was to remain so for another 17 years until acquired by the Transport Holding Company before it was absorbed by the newly created National Bus Company in 1969.

The last Bullock buses were withdrawn from West Riding service in 1968. A survivor is CHL 772 (342), a 1950 Willowbrook-bodied single-deck Daimler CVD6, which is part of a vintage fleet working in Somerset. Barnaby-bodied Leyland PS1 single-decker AHL 694 (284) of 1947 vintage is also fully restored and based in Northumberland. All the purpose-built depots in Wakefield (2), Featherstone and Selby that passed to West Riding have been demolished in recent times. Doncaster remains as a retail showroom. The original head office area in Wilson Street, Featherstone, has been redeveloped but still retains the original and still active B & S Sports and Social Club; all that remains of the local company that lost its identity over 50 years ago.

South Yorkshire Road Transport Ltd

Above: May Winder, the proprietor of the South Yorkshire Motor Company, is seen in Templar Street, Leeds, about to step into one of her Studebaker coaches for London. Tommy Barr is the confident-looking driver. This may have been the first journey made in 1927. South Yorkshire was the first company to operate a road service from Leeds to London.

Below: South Yorkshire eventually operated four Studebaker 'Big Six' vehicles, as shown below, which were used on the London service. They also appeared on the Pontefract to Doncaster stage-carriage services but proved costly to maintain and did not have a long life. *(Both: SYRT)*

Above: **WX 1531** (**29**), a 1929 20-seat Reo Speed Wagon with Harrison of Dewsbury coachwork, is shown parked outside the South Yorkshire Motors Cornmarket premises. It was one of five Reos obtained under the new management.

Below: **UA 464** (**19**) was a 1927 Dennis E with Ramsden of Liversedge 32-seat body. It was one of seven Dennis E- and F-types taken over from Winders. It is doubtful any were used on the London service. Most were withdrawn after five years' use. *(Both: SYRT)*

Above and below: **WX 2038** (**34**) of 1929 was an Albion Viking PMA28 model fitted with a 26-seat body, believed to be by NCME, with coach seating for the London service. This was one of the first Albions in the long association of this manufacturer with South Yorkshire extending 30 years, and it set a luxurious seating standard that would be seen on most future South Yorkshire vehicles. *(SYRT)*

Upper: **WX 2326** (**35**), a 1929 Albion Viking PMA26 with a 1943 Burlingham 32-seat utility body, is pictured in Marshgate bus station, Doncaster. It was in regular service until 1950 when it became a works transport until 1956, giving it a much longer life than its sister buses of the same era. *(David Allen Collection)*

Centre and Lower: **WX 3756** (**39**), a 1930 Albion Viking PMA28 fitted with coachwork showing English Electric features as rebodied by South Yorkshire in 1938. It was withdrawn in 1946. *(SYRT; H-S Transport Collection)*

Above: **WW 7619** (**45**) was a 1928 Leyland PLSC3 Lion 31-seater, one of two which came from the Hallamshire Transport Co. It was originally numbered 26. Rebodied and renumbered by South Yorkshire in 1935, it is seen on the 'fairground' at the rear of the Cornmarket garage in Pontefract at that time. It finished its days in 1944 and went to a showman in Wigton.

Below: **AWR 581** (**44**). This 1935 Albion Valkyrie SpPW67 with a 31-seat English Electric body is again posing on the 'fairground'. It was withdrawn in 1951 and sold to builders in Knottingley. *(Both: John Lambert Collection)*

Above: A Ford Recovery truck was acquired in 1936 when South Yorkshire became a Ford Main Dealer of cars, trucks and agricultural tractors in Pontefract followed by dealerships in Wakefield and later in Castleford. The Ford relationship was kept and developed over the next 40 years against the bus side of the business that remained mostly static. *(John Lambert Collection)*

Below: Proudly standing on Marine Drive, Scarborough in June 1934 is **YG 8207** (**42**). A 1934 Albion Valkyrie SpPW67, its English Electric body, complete with curtains, was to a design somewhat similar to contemporary Leyland coachwork. The Albion was to receive a Burlingham utility body during the war, but was withdrawn shortly afterwards in 1946. Behind is a Hoyles of Halifax Leyland Cheetah. *(G H F Atkins/© John Banks Collection)*

Above: **BWY 438** (**47**), a 1937 Albion Valkyrie SpPW141 with 31-seat English Electric body. This was the first Albion to have a Gardner 5LW engine, earlier vehicles having Gardner 4LW units. WX 7861 (40), a 20-seat Albion Victor, even had a Gardner 3LW as original equipment. Number 47 was withdrawn in 1957, going to the Wakefield Shirt Company as works transport. *(David Allen Collection)*

Below: **CWW 374** (**49**) was a 1938 Albion Valkyrie CX11 fitted with 35-seat Burlingham coachwork. The paint style adopted for this coach was an exception within the fleet. Withdrawn in 1957, it also saw further work with the Wakefield Shirt Company. *(Roger Holmes)*

Above: **DYG 53 (51)**, a 1941 Albion Valkyrie CX13 with Duple coachwork, was of a type that the Red and White company was taking in some number. It is seen in Marshgate bus station, Doncaster. By all accounts, fitted with the all-new Albion EN 242 9.08-litre engine, this was a speedy machine. It was the subject of a body change (Burlingham) from JWT 112 in 1958 and renumbered 57. *(Roger Holmes)*

Below: **DYG 53 (57)**, the 1941 Albion Valkyrie CX13 illustrated above as No. 51, is seen here with the 1950 33-seat Burlingham coachwork fitted to it in 1958. The vehicle has been faithfully restored and can be regularly seen at commercial vehicle rallies. *(David Allen Collection)*

Upper: **EWX 569** (**60**), a 1946 Albion Valkyrie CX13 with 34-seat Pickering body. Hostilities over, South Yorkshire quickly managed to secure three of these buses to replace the ageing 1929 Viking PMA28 vehicles. Number 60 is seen in Central bus station, Leeds, giving a nearside view with the unusual illuminated 'duplicate' sign. *(Alan Cross)*

Centre: **EWX 569** (**60**) again. It is seen this time outside the Cornmarket premises giving an offside view emphasising the austerity type bodywork of the period from the Scottish coachbuilder in Wishaw. It was withdrawn in 1957 and, like some of its stable mates, joined the Wakefield Shirt Company. (*R F Mack/David Allen Collection*)

Lower: **GWT 630** (**61**), a 1947 Albion Valkyrie CX13, came with 33-seat Burlingham coachwork and is shown here in Central bus station, Leeds. It did not have an intensive service life and as a consequence lasted some 20 years with South Yorkshire in its original state before passing into preservation. *(David Allen Collection)*

Above: South Yorkshire had an active body shop until the reformation of the Company in 1973. In this print we see English Electric-bodied Albions being renovated. The figure in the centre of the picture is believed to be Bernard Thompson, a member of the engineering staff for many years.

Below: The interior of the Cornmarket premises was quite spacious and buses shared the area with new Ford cars as shown in this mid 1950s print. Albion coach **GWT 630 (61)** is under the vehicle wash, and coach **JWT 112 (57)** is also shown before being rebuilt as a double-decker and reregistered **TWY 8 (81)** in 1958. *(Both: SYRT)*

Above: **EWT 954** (**52**), a 1943 Daimler CWA6 with 55-seat Duple utility body stands on the 'fairground'. This was the first double-deck bus in the fleet. Three others also arrived - some fifteen years after other companies in the area introduced them. A rare rear view of **EWU 772** (**55**), a 1944 Daimler CWA6 with Brush utility body, and a Pickering bodied Albion, **EWX 568** (**59**). All had been withdrawn from service by 1960. *(Roger Holmes)*

Below: **EWT 956** (**53**), a 1944 Daimler CWA6 with 55-seat Brush utility body (reduced to 53 shortly after entering service), stands in Selby Market Place. It was operating on the service from Pontefract via Whitley Bridge running only on Saturday, Sunday and Monday (market day). In the last years of South Yorkshire operation, this service terminated at Whitley Bridge. *(The Omnibus Society)*

Above: Another view of **EWT 954** (**52**), the 1943 Daimler CWA6 with Duple bodywork. It was in Beastfair, Pontefract, one of the terminal points in the town before the bus station was opened. The bus was withdrawn from service in 1960. *(Alan Cross)*

Below: Albion's independent bus building days were numbered when these three Venturer CX37S models arrived in 1950 with Strachan 55-seat bodies. **JWT 873-5** (**70-2**) had, by the time of this photograph, undergone some heavy body refurbishment - not uncommon with this coachbuilder's products at that time. They had been withdrawn from service by 1967. *(R F Mack/John Lambert Collection)*

Above: **GWT 631** (**56**), a 1947 Strachan-bodied Albion Venturer CX19, was parked in Cornmarket, Pontefract. This bus heralded a return to the Albion product for the growing double-deck fleet after the enforced wartime purchase of Daimlers. The original strong Strachan body/paint lines are in evidence in this picture. *(R F Mack/John Lambert Collection)*

Below: **JWR 874** (**71**), a 1950 Albion Venturer CX37S, again Strachan-bodied, in a rear view of the familiar style of this manufacturer who supplied a significant number of bodies to the industry in the immediate postwar period. *(John Fozard Collection)*

Above: Nineteen-fifty Strachan-bodied Albion Venturer CX37S **JWR 875** (**72**) stands in Selby Market Place on the thrice-weekly service to Pontefract through Whitley Bridge. Bullocks/West Riding also operated a daily service to Pontefract from Selby via Monk Fryston. *(David Allen Collection)*

Below: **TWY 8** (**81**) was the 1950 Albion Valiant CX39N with 1958 Roe 55-seat body that started out life as JWT 112 with a Burlingham coach body. It was rebodied and reregistered and is now preserved with the distinction of being the only known double-deck Valiant bus in existence. Because of its rarity, it became something of an icon with local bus enthusiasts up to its withdrawal in the 1960s. The picture was taken in Marshgate bus station, Doncaster. *(R F Mack/John Lambert Collection)*

<< Opposite page: A view in Marshgate bus station, Doncaster, of **JWR 873** (**70**), a 1950 Albion Venturer CX37S, shows in detail the original Strachan body before refurbishment altered its appearance, most notably by heavy rubber mouldings around the windows. It was withdrawn in 1965 and was another sale to the Wakefield Shirt Company. *(G H F Atkins/© John Banks Collection)*

This page: **KWU 978** (**73**) was one of four 1951 Leyland Titan PD2/12s fitted with the chassis maker's own bodywork. *(John Banks Collection)*

<< Opposite page: This mid-sixties scene shows **KWY 224** (**76**), a 1951 Leyland PD2, approaching Selby on a market day. Each Monday when markets were held all bus services were diverted from the Market Place to Park Street some distance away. This arrangement lasted until Selby bus station was opened in June 1969. On Bank Holiday Mondays, both South Yorkshire and West Riding ran many extra buses into Selby from surrounding areas for this popular market day event. *(Alan Cross)*

Above: **KWU 978** (**73**), a 1951 Leyland PD2, is shown leaving Marshgate bus station. This and its three sister vehicles were the mainstay of South Yorkshire's longer services for a number of years.

Below: **KWY 223** (**75**), another of the same batch, pulls up at Whitwood Technical College, near Castleford, on the route from Doncaster to Leeds. *(Both: David Allen Collection)*

Above: The final development of the halfcab bus began in the mid-fifties when the concealed radiator or 'tin front' became the fashion. **OWR 264 (77)**, a 1954 Leyland PD2/20 with Bond bodywork, and a similar bus were the first such vehicles in the fleet. Seen here running into Leeds at Thwaite Gate, 77 - known by staff as the 'Sunset Strip' after the popular TV series of the day - had platform doors and fluorescent strip-lighting. This set the standard for future South Yorkshire vehicles. *(Alan Cross)*

Below: The next pair of Leyland Titans came in 1957. One of them, **TWY 6 (79)**, a Park Royal-bodied PD2/20, was at Marshgate, Doncaster. Alongside is West Riding **BHL 801 (654)**, a 1948 Leyland PD2/1 highbridge type operating from Selby depot. *(David Allen Collection)*

Above: **TWY 6** (**79**) is seen again, in Leeds Central bus station awaiting its return trip to Doncaster. A Yorkshire Woollen coach is parked in the background. *(David Allen Collection)*

Below: South Yorkshire purchased two Roe-bodied Leyland PD3/1 buses in 1960, one of which was **2600 WW** (**83**) pictured at Thwaite Gate, Leeds. These were the last halfcab buses to enter the fleet. With an increased length of 30 feet and seating capacity of 63, these lowbridge buses had a sleek appearance. However, only a few of this model were ever sold. The sunken gangway upstairs had never been popular, and was no longer necessary with the new generation of buses arriving such as the rear-engined Leyland Atlantean. The last South Yorkshire halfcab buses were withdrawn in the late nineteen seventies. *(Alan Cross)*

<< *Opposite page:* At Marshgate, Doncaster, South Yorkshire buses represent three distinct development periods of the double-decker. Centre-stage is **KWY 223 (75)**, a 1951 Leyland PD2/12 basically unchanged in design since Leyland introduced the halfcab bus in the late 1920s. The concealed radiator or 'tin front' of the mid 1950s is seen on the right on **2599 WW (82)**, a 1960 Roe-bodied Leyland PD3/1 - the final development of the traditional halfcab bus. On the left is **391 CWT (85)**, a 1963 Weymann-bodied Leyland Atlantean PDR1/1 representing the rear-engined buses which came on stream in the early 1960s giving a much increased passenger capacity, and of a layout still in vogue forty years later. Also visible is a West Riding 1961 AEC Reliance Roe one-man-operated bus. *(David Allen Collection)*

This page upper: The first two Leyland PDR1/1 Atlanteans arrived in 1963. They had the low height Weymann body with the usual South Yorkshire high standard seating specification for 70 passengers. **391 CWT (85)** is seen in Leeds Central bus station showing the revised livery of the reformed company of 1973. *(David Allen Collection)*

Centre: YWX 402X (102/505) 1982 Leyland Olympian ONTL11/1R with Northern Counties 71-seat body pulls out of Pontefract bus station in early Caldaire days on local service 487 in April 1995. This was one of the first Olympians to be sold to a private company, and one of a number for the South Yorkshire fleet in the 1980s. It was withdrawn in 1996. *(David Allen Collection)*

Lower: Ex-Park's of Hamilton 1973 Volvo coach **LVD 815L (15)**, with Plaxton Elite coachwork, in Pontefract in use on the short-lived Manchester express service. It was withdrawn in 1982. *(H-S Transport Collection)*

Upper: A surprise purchase in 1975 was of two 1969 ex-Yorkshire Woollen Marshall-bodied AEC Reliance buses. Not only were they the first single-deck stage carriage vehicles to be obtained for many years, but the first second-hand service buses, although a number of used coaches had been bought. **KCP 809G** (**9**) is shown. Both were withdrawn in 1980. *(David Allen Collection)*

Centre: Coaches began to join the fleet in 1973; almost all were Leyland or Volvo. At Northgate depot are **OWT 1M** (**1**), a 1973 Volvo B58 with Duple 53 seat coachwork - the first purchased after the company was reformed, and **LWW 5P** (**5**), a similar vehicle dating from 1975. These coaches were sold in 1979 and 1983. *(David Allen Collection)*

Lower: A participant in the 26th British Coach Rally in Brighton was **MUM 318V** (**18**), a 1980 Volvo B58 with Caetano 53-seat coachwork. This was at a time when South Yorkshire was developing the coaching side of the business and entered a coach in the Brighton rally on more than one occasion. *(John Banks Collection)*

J Bullock & Sons (1928) Ltd

Above: Jim Bullock poses at the wheel of his first charabanc in 1909 - a chain driven 15-seat Karrier. The photograph is believed to have been taken in Huddersfield where Jim was given a month's training by the Karrier company. The vehicle was requisitioned by the War Department in 1914 and was never returned. *(WROPS)*

Below: This unidentified charabanc could be on its way to one of two ordnance factories at Horbury or Crossgates, Leeds during the First World War. Bullocks were allowed to keep one or two non-requisitoned vehicles for this purpose. 'Abe' Bullock is the driver. *(John Lambert Collection)*

Above: **U 3204** was a 1913 Austin 2/3-ton 18-seat charabanc, pictured at a comfort stop (in the real meaning) at Scagglethorpe, today bypassed by the A64. The driver was George Speight, who went on to become one of the longest-serving Bullocks employees. The vehicle was probably the second to be acquired by Bullocks. Travelling to Scarborough from Featherstone in such a vehicle in those days must have been an adventure, especially in a solid-tyred vehicle lacking one headlight and a door. This vehicle had been withdrawn by 1921. *(John Lambert Collection)*

Below: **WU 1441 (5)**, a 1925 Halley 3½ ton 26-seat bus, seen with driver Norman Pickersgill, was only a year old when Healds of Normanton were taken over by Bullocks in 1926. Records show that as an economy measure on takeover the 'H' on the side of the bus was simply changed to 'B' by Bullocks, the Healds basic colour scheme being not dissimilar from the Bullocks red. *(John Lambert Collection)*

Above: **WT 4821** (**12**), a 1924 Leyland GH7 with 30-seat Strachan and Brown body, is seen at the B & S 'Motor Station' which was at the rear of the Black Swan Hotel in Vicar Lane, Leeds. The three Featherstone-based crew are believed to be Inspector Flowers, Driver Freddie Blackburn and Conductor Norman Wrigglesworth. A notice makes it clear 'that passengers cannot be picked up or set down in the city'. This bus was withdrawn by 1932 and like many other passenger vehicles of the day, was sold and converted for the carriage of goods. *(SYRT)*

Below: The clarity of this print clearly shows the features of **HL 2669** (**14**), a 1925 Leyland A13 with Strachan and Brown 28-seat body, as it stands in Pontefract Market Place. Horace Lawrence was the driver, Sid Armstrong the young conductor. The bus later saw further service with the Blyth and Berwick company in Bradford before eventual conversion to a truck in the late nineteen thirties. *(John Lambert Collection)*

Above: **WY 8958** (**22**), a1923 Leyland RAF type with Strachan and Brown body, meets **HL 2181** (**37**), a 1924 Lancia with a Bell body. **WY 8958** was still running on solid tyres when most of the fleet had been converted. The print appears to be a publicity shot highlighting road problems of the day. Nothing changes. Both vehicles were withdrawn when the company was reformed in 1928. *(David Allen Collection)*

Below: The first Selby depot was established on the Holmes in the mid 1920s when J W Smith of Osgodby was taken over. **WW 7378** (**40**), a 1928 Albion SpLC 24 fitted with a Bell body taken from a 1924 Lancia, is shown parked at the depot. *(SYRT)*

Above: **HL 4346** (**43**) was a 1929 AEC Reliance, believed fitted with a 32-seat Barnsley Motors body. Joe Ash was the driver and the photograph was taken at Old Church Pontefract. This was one of two Reliance buses bought at the time. AEC produced this model as a stop gap 1920s design until the popular and long-lived Regal model, of which Bullocks ordered two, appeared later that year. *(John Lambert Collection)*

Below: Sovereign Street, Leeds, was the terminus for some of the Bullocks services for many years. Here **WW 5494** (**77**), a 1928 Albion PM28 with Clark 30-seat body awaits departure for Hemsworth. It left the company in 1935 and went to a showman. Lister Edwards of Featherstone is the conductor. *(David Allen Collection)*

Above: Clark of Scunthorpe produced a number of bodies for Bullocks in 1928 on Leyland or Albion chassis. This factory picture shows **WW 6768** (**78**), a 1928 Albion PM28, before delivery. Note the unusual position of the spare wheel. The bus was scrapped in the late 1930s.

Below: This Leyland Lion PLSC3 was one of two, WW 6771/2 (86/7), bodied by Clark in 1928. On this chassis the spare wheel was hidden. Both buses were withdrawn in 1940. One at least ran with a subsequent owner until 1948. *(Both: SYRT)*

Above: **HL 3902** (**83**) was a 1928 Leyland Lion PLSC3 and was an all-Leyland product with a 35-seat body. This model led the way in bus design and made Leyland a household name in the bus business. It was to be seen in all parts of the country and Bullocks ordered six. They had all been withdrawn by the late 1930s. Most were converted to trucks or showmen's vehicles and worked until the late 1940s. *(David Allen Collection)*

Below: **HL 3192** (**89**), a 1926 Leyland Lion PLSC1 was another early all Leyland product. The PLSC1 was a shorter version of the PLSC3. The vehicle is seen at Featherstone after being rebodied in 1934, probably by Barnsley Bodies. It was originally fleet number 59. Withdrawn from service in 1937, it was scrapped in 1943. *(John Lambert Collection)*

Upper: As with many fledgling companies at this time, Leyland had a growing presence in the Bullocks fleet, which acquired its first double-deck bus in 1931. **HL5072 (118)**, a Leyland Titan TD1 with 51-seat bodywork by the chassis maker, is seen before delivery. It gave fourteen years of service before passing to a Leeds showman who kept it until 1954.

Centre and Lower: **HL 4460 (97)** was a 1929 all Leyland Tiger TS2 model, again photographed in as-built condition. Refurbished or possibly rebodied in 1935 it was renumbered as No. 183. Withdrawn in 1940, it had a number of owners in the Leeds area before being scrapped in 1952. *(All: John Banks Collection)*

Upper: **HL 4743** (**113**), a 1930 Daimler CF6 with Taylors of Barnsley 30-seat coachwork (note the curtains) is seen on Marine Drive, Scarborough. This was one of two identical coaches - the first new generation Daimlers in a growing mixed fleet. Both had short lives with Bullocks going to Farsley Omnibus Company in 1936. 113 was eventually scrapped in Leeds in 1945.

Centre: In another Marine Drive view was **HL 4770** (**114**), a 1930 Plaxton-bodied AEC Regal 32-seater, again one of a pair purchased in 1930. Both had canvas folding roofs and could pass under the low railway bridge at Rawcliffe. By 1940 both had been withdrawn from service. 114 ended its days in London in 1956. *(Both: G H F Atkins/© John Banks Collection)*

Lower: The first Leyland Titan TD2 model arrived in 1932. **HL 5642** (**147**) was a 1933 example. The exhaust smoke suggests a recent

cold start. Not being rebuilt in its lifetime like other early Titans, it was withdrawn from service in 1949 and passed to a Beverley showman and was scrapped in 1954. *(David Allen Collection)*

Above: Roberts of Horbury produced this rear-entrance coach on **HL 5774** (**154**), a Daimler CP6, in 1933. It had a short life with Bullocks, going to Farsley Omnibus Company in 1937, with whom it remained until 1952. *(The Wakefield Collection)*

Below: Bullocks had at least six buses requisitioned for War Department use in 1940. **HL 5423** (**135**), a 1932 AEC Regal with a Taylor 32-seat body, was fitted out as a mobile theatre by the Wakefield Entertainments Committee and probably used by E.N.S.A. The gentleman seems pleased with the result. The bus did not return to Bullocks but finished up with an Ely showman in 1945. *(WROPS)*

Upper: Driver Horace Lawrence appears deservedly proud of his smart steed, **HL 5813 (157)**, a 1933 Leyland LT5 Burlingham-bodied 32-seater with roof luggage carrier - necessary for the Blackpool services - and sliding roof. The high standard of upholstery, akin to that of a railway coach of the period, is evident. The vehicle was rebodied by Barnaby in 1946 and survived into West Riding ownership. *(John Lambert Collection)*

Centre and lower: Standardisation was not a word in the Bullock vocabulary. Five more Daimlers appeared in 1934 among the AECs and Leylands. One was **HL 6095 (158)**, a Roberts-bodied 1934 Daimler CP6. It is seen before and after delivery in these views, in the lower picture at Marine Drive, Scarborough. Rebuilt by Bullocks in 1941, it was withdrawn in 1947 and gave further service to a York operator for three months. *(The Wakefield Collection; G H F Atkins/© John Banks Collection)*

Above: **HL 6268 (161)**, a 1934 AEC Q with Weymann 39-seat body, was the petrol version of two similar vehicles purchased. This one operated from Wakefield depot, the other being diesel was based at Featherstone. This revolutionary model never realised its potential and gave a certain amount of trouble; the above example was scrapped in 1943. The diesel bus (162) was returned to AEC soon after entering service, survived for a few years with a Welsh operator and was scrapped in 1939. *(Alan Townsin Collection)*

Below: Bullocks buses are well in evidence in this period scene taken in Selby about 1950. All had been withdrawn from service by 1955. **HL 5583 (144)**, a 1932 all Leyland Titan TD2, had recently been rebuilt and is seen leaving the Market Place. It was withdrawn in 1953 and scrapped. The single-decker was **HL 6397 (160)**, a 1934 Leyland LT5A with Barnaby 32-seat body also rebuilt by NMU at York. It spent most of its life at Selby depot coming out of service in 1952. The other double-decker was an austerity (utility) bus, **AHL 30 (263)**, a 1944 Daimler CWA6 with a Duple angled-dome body. It is remembered for its uncomfortable lightly covered slatted-wood seating. Withdrawn in 1955, it gave further service to a London operator until 1958. The two Jowett vehicles in the Market Place (a Bradford pickup belonging to Northern Dairies and a Javelin car) help to date this view. *(David Allen Collection)*

Upper and Centre: **HL 6584** (**173**), a 1935 all-Leyland TD3 is shown in brand new condition. All of 1935's purchases for the Bullocks fleet were Leylands, HL 6584 being the only double-decker among nine vehicles delivered. It developed the notorious structural defects of the early Leyland metal-framed body, which Barnaby replaced during the war. The bus survived the West Riding takeover and went to a building contractor in 1953. It was scrapped in 1957.

Below: Another of the 1935 Leylands was **HL 6585** (**174**), a Lion LT7 model, seen here before delivery. Used as an ambulance during the war, it was rebodied by Bullocks in 1944 and withdrawn immediately after the West Riding takeover. It saw further service with a showman until 1957. *(All: John Banks Collection)*

Upper and centre: **HL 6288** (**163**), a 1934
Leyland Lion LT5A with Roberts 32-seat body,
was one of a number of buses equipped by the
Horbury coachbuilder. It is seen here before
delivery. This was another vehicle rebodied by
Barnaby in 1946. It was withdrawn shortly after
the West Riding takeover and worked for a
showman until 1960. *(Senior Transport Archive;
The Wakefield Collection)*

Lower: **HL 6292** (**167**), another 1934 Leyland
Lion LT5A lost its Roberts body in 1946 and is
seen with its replacement Barnaby body in Leeds
Central bus station. It was withdrawn in 1953 and
scrapped. Adjacent is West Riding **HL 6637**
(**411**) 1935 Leyland TS7c of similar vintage used
as an ambulance during the war and then
rebodied by Roe. *(Alan Cross)*

Above: **HL 4347** (**95**), a 1929 Leyland Tiger TS2 is shown at Scarborough, a popular destination for Yorkshire excursionists, with its original 32-seat body of unknown make: possibly Leyland or Taylor. This was one of four Leyland models purchased in that year. *(John Banks Collection)*

Below: In 1935 the bus was rebodied by Barnaby of Hull and renumbered (**182**). This was the start of the Bullocks association with Barnaby. In 1939 the bus passed to the War Department. It was not returned to Bullocks and was withdrawn from use in 1948. *(David Allen Collection)*

HL 7072 (185), a 1936 Daimler CP6 with Brush 32-seat coachwork was a Commercial Motor Show exhibit. Brush was a new coachwork supplier to Bullocks and this was a luxurious vehicle, which remained in use until 1948. It then passed to a York operator before becoming a cricket pavilion at Appleton Roebuck until the 1950s. Special Daimler Show markings are prominent in the bottom photograph. *(David Allen Collection)*

Upper and centre: During 1934 Roberts of Horbury provided coachwork on a number of Leyland and Daimler chassis for Bullocks. **HL 6291 (166)**, a 1934 Leyland Lion LT5A is shown as new before entering service. *(Senior Archive; The Wakefield Collection)*

Lower: Willowbrook provided the unusual double-deck coachwork on two 1934 Daimler COG5 chassis with enclosed saloons. Upstairs a twin aisle was provided giving a lower seating capacity of forty-eight. **HL 6349 (171)** is seen when new. Ten years later 171 and sister bus 170 were rebuilt by Barnaby with traditional-style 53-seat bodies. Both were withdrawn in early West Riding days. *(John Lambert Collection)*

Above: **HL 7406 (188)**, a 1936 AEC Regal/Duple 32-seat coach, was the first of three similar stylish coaches. Rebuilt by Bullocks in 1949, it ran on stage-carriage services well into the West Riding era and was withdrawn in 1955. It is photographed above in its final days at Belle Isle, Wakefield. *(R F Mack/David Allen Collection)*

Below: **HL 7414 (195)** was a 1936 Daimler CP6 with Bullock 32-seat coachwork. It was the pride of the fleet for some years. Built by the Company's own craftsmen at Featherstone, it incorporated many luxury features such as concealed lighting, Australian silky oak interior woodwork, and smart stainless steel and chrome fittings. As with many of the coaches, 195 was put into storage each winter. It was withdrawn in 1948 and ran for a number of other operators before being scrapped in 1951. *(John Lambert Collection)*

Upper and Centre: Seen before delivery is **HL 7415** (**196**), a 1936 all-Leyland Tiger TS7 32-seat bus, one of two Leyland products purchased that year with metal-framed bodies (the other being a double-decker). In 1940 it was requisitioned for ambulance duties at Featherstone and later rebodied as a coach by Barnaby. It ran into the West Riding era, being withdrawn in 1951. By 1956 it was noted still working for a showman. *(Both: John Banks Collection).*

Lower: **HL 7771** (**198**), a 1936 AEC Regal with Barnaby 32-seat service-bus bodywork, is seen in July 1953 during its final days as the depot tow vehicle at Selby. Barnaby had rebodied this vehicle in 1943. Withdrawn in 1953, it survived with a showman until 1957. *(David Allen)*

Above: **HL 7772 (199)** was one of two identical 1937 Willowbrook-bodied AEC Regents delivered in that year. They had a relatively low seating capacity of 48, like previous Willowbrook products. Both were refurbished by Barnaby in 1945 but did not have a long life, being withdrawn by 1951. *(John Lambert Collection)*

Below: Standing in Cornmarket, Pontefract, is **HL 8058 (204)**, a Roe-bodied 1937 Leyland Tiger TS7. This bus originally had Duple coachwork as did two identical Leylands. The replacement Roe body was fitted to 204 in 1949 and the vehicle was withdrawn from service in 1961. *(Alan Cross)*

Above: Parked on Marine Drive, Scarborough, is **HL 8064** (**210**), a 1937 Leyland Tiger TS7 with Barnaby 32-seat coachwork. It carried the new style of coach motif on the vehicle sides and was refurbished by Bullocks in 1944. Along with other Leylands of a similar age, it received a new Longford coach body in 1949 and was renumbered (344). It had a long service life and was not withdrawn until 1963. *(David Allen Collection)*

Below: **HL 8494** (**217**), a 1937 Roe-bodied AEC Regent, stands in Wakefield bus station in West Riding days. It was one of two AEC Regents placed in service at the same time and spent much of its Bullock service working out of their small Doncaster depot. It was withdrawn in 1961. *(R F Mack/David Allen Collection)*

Upper: After the problems with metal-framed bodywork in the early nineteen-thirties, Leyland changed the design and produced the attractive double-deck body style shown on **HL 8652** (**219**), a 1938 Titan TD5. *(John Banks Collection)*

Centre: **HL 8493** (**216**), a 1937 AEC Regent, had a seating capacity of 48 compared with the 53 or 55 usually found in a lowbridge double-deck body. This order for two lowbridge AEC Regents was the first order placed by Bullocks with local coachbuilder Charles H Roe, of Crossgates, Leeds. *(John Banks Collection)*

Lower: **HL 9171** (**228**), a 1938 Roe-bodied Leyland Titan TD5 stands in Central bus station, Leeds. Originally equipped with 48 seats, it was one of a pair ordered. It was later reseated to 53 and remained in service until 1957. *(David Allen Collection)*

Above: Two stylish Barnaby 32-seat coach bodies were built on Leyland Tiger TS8 chassis in 1938. One of them, **HL 8814 (222)**, is seen as built.

Below: **HL 8814** had a long and varied life and lasted into the West Riding period. It was rebuilt by Barnaby in 1946 and rebodied in 1956 with the Willowbrook body taken from Leyland PS1 Tiger AHL 810 (301) as seen at Belle Isle. When withdrawn in 1962, it had achieved 24 years continuous service. *(Both: David Allen Collection)*

Above: **HL 9494** (**232**), a 1939 Daimler COG5 with Willowbrook coachwork, was a 39-seat dual-purpose bus, one of four Willowbrook-bodied buses bought in that year including two small Bedford WTB coaches. It is seen in Central bus station, Leeds, with its refurbished body completed by Barnaby in 1948. It was withdrawn from service and scrapped in 1954. The body, however, saw further service on a Samuel Ledgard 1935 Leyland TS7 - BUA 402 - until 1958. *(T W Moore)*

Below: **HL 9464** (**234**), a 1939 Barnaby-bodied 32-seat Leyland Tiger TS8 coach, stands in Market Place, Pontefract, in its later West Riding years on stage carriage services. Barnaby rebuilt the coach in 1949, which continued in service until 1953. *(Roger Holmes)*

Upper and Centre: Bullocks managed to secure seven Leyland buses in 1940 before prewar production was halted. **HL 9806** (**241**), a 1940 all-Leyland Titan TD7 was the first of a pair delivered in March. In 1961 it was among the last of the prewar Bullock buses to be withdrawn from service. *(Both: John Banks Collection)*

Lower: **HL 9882** (**247**), a 1940 Leyland Tiger TS8 with Barnaby body, was the last of the prewar specification buses to arrive and the only single-decker of that year. Refurbished by Cawood in 1948, it is seen here in its later years at Featherstone. It was last used in service during 1956. *(David Allen Collection)*

<< *Opposite page upper:* With the country at war, constraints and changes were inevitable. **HL 9808** (**243**), a 1940 Leyland Titan TD7 with Roe bodywork, was one of the last prewar buses to be received. It was immediately fitted with headlamp masks and white markings. It was withdrawn in 1961. *(John Lambert Collection)*

<< *Opposite page lower:* The first austerity (utility) buses arrived in 1942. **HL 9990** (**255**), a 1943 Guy Arab I with sluggish Gardner 5LW engine, came a year later. It was allocated to Selby Depot where it remained until withdrawn from service in 1951 and is seen here in Selby Market Place. As with many other buses, it was painted grey for the latter period of the war. *(Alan Cross)*

Above: Bullocks managed to obtain more Daimlers than Guys during the hostilities. Only a few coachbuilders were authorised to build utility-specification bodywork and Brush was one. **AHL 35** (**266**) was a 1944 Daimler CWA6, photographed at Thwaite Gate on its way into Leeds looking the worse for wear towards the end of its service life which came in 1955. *(John Lambert Collection)*

Above: Daimlers remained favourites after the War, or perhaps operators had to take what they could get before vehicle production returned to normal after the early postwar period of austerity and shortages. **AHL 392 (273)**, a 1946 Duple-bodied Daimler CWD6, was photographed in Park Street, Selby, the terminus for bus services on Monday market days at that time. A number of Daimler double-deckers came during the year with either Duple or Strachan bodywork.

Below: **AHL 453 (278)**, another 1946 Daimler CWD6, had Strachan bodywork. It was parked in Market Place, Pontefract not long before its 1961 withdrawal. *(Both: John Fozard Collection)*

Above: Among the Daimlers purchased immediately after the war were two single-deckers with coachwork by Barnaby. One was **AHL 560 (281)**, a 1946 CVD6 35-seat dual-purpose bus, seen in this picture at rest in Central bus station, Leeds. It lasted only seven years in service before disposal in 1953. *(J B Parkin)*

Below: Leylands began to reappear in 1947 with a large batch of Tiger PS1 single-deckers. Barnaby and Willowbrook shared the coachwork requirements. **AHL 698 (288)**, a Barnaby 35-seater, was one of this batch and it is seen here in 1960 at Wakefield in West Riding days before disposal in 1962. *(Roger Holmes)*

Upper: AHL 695 (285), a Leyland Tiger PS1/Barnaby, was another of the early postwar acquisitions. It was in service until 1963, and like many other buses of the day was photographed in Central bus station, Leeds. *(WROPS)*

Centre: BHL 242 (304) from the 1947 intake of Leyland PS1 Tigers had Willowbrook bodywork. It is seen outside the Savile Street Depot in Wakefield showing the Bullock motif usually placed on coaches at that time. *(Senior Transport Archive)*

Lower: AHL 809 (300), another of the 1947 Leyland PS1s bodied by Willowbrook, is parked with similar buses at Scarborough in July 1950 on excursion duties. In 1956 West Riding took an unusual step in having twelve of the PSls, including this one, fitted with Roe double-deck bodies which gave them a further ten years or so of service life. The exercise overcame a pressing shortage of double-deck capacity at that time. *(G H F Atkins/© John Banks Collection)*

Above: By 1947, early postwar conditions of austerity were easing: double-deckers to postwar standard designs were becoming available and Bullocks ordered six AEC Regent IIIs from Roe. **AHL 927 (295)** was in Central bus station, Leeds, in August 1949. Like most of the batch it worked most of its early service life from Featherstone depot. They were all withdrawn in 1963.

Below: **BHL 194 (308)**, a 1947 Daimler CVD6 bodied by Strachan, was one of a batch of three similar buses in that year; body structural problems gave them a short life. Number 308 was photographed in August 1949 in Leeds and was scrapped in 1955. *(Both: G H F Atkins/© John Banks Collection)*

Above: **BHL 195** (**309**), a 1947 Daimler CVD6 bodied by Strachan, was photographed in Castleford bus station in West Riding days, It had had the windows and surrounds modified, which no doubt lengthened its life to 1959. This can be compared with sister bus 308 shown as delivered on page 71.

Below: **BHL 272** (**313**), a 1947 all-Leyland PD2, shown in Leeds, was the first of the batch of six that arrived at the end of the year. This completed one of the largest vehicle-buying programmes Bullocks had undertaken to recover from the war years. Behind is a West Riding 1950 Leyland PD2 **DHL 151** (**704**), which had been part of a Bullocks order that was completed after the takeover. *(Both: Alan Cross)*

Above: This familiar setting in Leeds shows **CHL 233** (**325**), a 1948 Daimler CVD6/Roe, on the stand for the long route to Goole via Selby. This bus and 323 from the same batch were allocated new to Selby depot whose vehicles operated this service.

Below: Bullocks operated an all-year-round express service to Blackpool from Wakefield and surrounding areas. **CHL 273** (**332**), a 1949 AEC Regal III with Longford coachwork, is seen here in Westgate, Wakefield, possibly on a private charter. Three AECs and two Leylands with Longford coachwork were the last new coaches to join the fleet before West Riding took over. By 1964, all had been withdrawn and most scrapped. *(Both: Alan Cross)*

Above: Parked in Wood Street, Wakefield when new is **CHL 744** (**338**) 1950 Leyland PD2, one of Bullocks last two double deck additions to the fleet. It was in service until 1967. *(Alan Cross)*

Below: One of two unusual additions to the fleet was **CHL 384** (**329**), a 1949 Guy Arab III/Roe 32-seat bus here depicted when new in the smart Bullocks livery. They were the last Roe-bodied buses to be bought and by 1965 both had been scrapped. *(David Allen Collection)*

Above: A pair of Daimler dual-purpose 35-seat buses were the last vehicles to arrive in May 1950, four months before Bullocks joined up with West Riding. **CHL 771/2 (341/2)** were 1950 Daimler CVD6/Willowbrook buses. They were photographed in West Riding livery in Scarborough on excursion work. *(R F Mack/David Allen Collection)*

Below: Bullocks' relationship with coachbuilders Longford continued through 1949/50. **CHL 721 (336)**, a 1939 Leyland TD5/Longford 33-seat coach was a rebuild and reregistration of HL 9723 (240), which had suffered a serious accident at Doncaster. Other prewar Leylands were rebodied in a similar fashion. This picture was taken in Wakefield bus station. *(Alan Cross)*

Above: Bullocks had a requirement for some lighter buses to replace the wartime Bedford OWBs mostly used in the rural areas around Selby and particularly over the restricted river bridge in Cawood. **DHL 550 (708)** was the last of four Seddon-bodied Seddons to be delivered to fulfil this requirement (two in 1949/50 and a further two after West Riding took over), and was photographed in Marshgate, Doncaster.

Below: **CHL 742 (335)** and **DHL 550 (708)** again, both with Seddon/W.M.I. 31-seat bodies, are parked at Selby Depot. *(Both: David Allen Collection)*

Above: **HL 8817** (**345**), a 1938 Leyland Tiger TS8 with Longford 33-seat coachwork had its new coach body fitted in 1949, as did a number of other prewar Leyland Tigers models. Here, it is seen standing at Selby depot.

Below: Bullocks' first purpose-built garage in Wakefield was in Savile Street in the early 1930s near the junction with York Street as photographed below. Previously they had used premises in nearby Providence Street from 1920. When the new larger garage was built in Savile Street, a few hundred yards away, the old garage became a body repair/paint shop and was finally abandoned in 1963. *(Both: David Allen Collection)*

Above: City Garage, as Bullocks called it, was built at the junction of Savile Street and Union Street, Wakefield, in the late 1930s to house most of the 50 buses allocated to it. One entrance and side of the garage bordered Borough Road as seen on the left, now the site of platform 1 of the new bus station.

Below: City Garage offices were on the Savile Street side of the garage. They housed a booking and general administration office as well as the normal garage facilities. *(Both John Churms Collection)*

Wilson Street, Featherstone, was the registered office and depot base of Bullocks. Garage facilities had been built here in the early 1920s to house the growing fleet. The extensive and prominent office block can be seen from these prints. About 100 buses were eventually based at Wilson Street. The depot also had a very active sports and social club. The family business had originally started from premises in Station Lane around the corner. In October 1984 West Riding vacated the site and the premises were demolished. Today a supermarket occupies the area, but the original B & S Sports and Social Club survives and is still active. *(All: John Churms Collection)*

This page: Selby depot was built and opened in Chimes Road in May 1936. It had accommodation for 20 vehicles, but as services developed there was a requirement for more than 30 buses. Bullocks had had a presence in the town since the 1920s when they took over a local company (Smiths of Osgodby). A base was established at that time on the Holmes which closed when the new premises were opened. *(John Churms Collection)*

>> *Opposite page upper:* The colour section starts with **HL 8494** (**217**), a 1937 AEC Regent I/Roe, seen parked in Wakefield in June 1960, a year before it was withdrawn after 23 years' service.

>> *Opposite page lower:* **HL 9806** (**241**) was a 1940 all Leyland Titan TD7, also photographed in 1960. It was outside the body shop in Savile Street, Wakefield, before it, too, was withdrawn in1961. *(Both: Roger Holmes)*

Colour Section (1) - Bullocks vehicles in West Riding livery

Above: Pictured in Leeds on a summer's day is **AHL 807 (298)**, a 1947 Leyland PS1/Willowbrook on a local service from Castleford. It was one of the few PS1s of a large batch not to be fitted with a double-deck body by West Riding in 1956. After withdrawal in 1963 it served as a works transport until scrapped in 1968. *(Malcolm King)*

Below: **CHL 232 (324)**, a 1949 Daimler CVD 6/Roe, awaits its crew at Marshgate bus station, Doncaster, in November 1961 for its return trip to Pontefract. It was withdrawn and scrapped with the rest of its batch of Daimlers in 1963. *(Roger Holmes)*

Above: Among the last coaches to be purchased by Bullocks was **CHL 274 (333)**, a 1949 AEC Regal III/Longford, pictured in November 1964, not long before its 1965 withdrawal from service. Longford did quite a bit of business with Bullocks in the final years. *(Roger Holmes)*

Below: An offside view of **CHL 721 (336)**. This 1939 Longford-bodied Leyland TD5 had been rebuilt as a coach from double-decker No. 240 in 1949 and reregistered. The coach spent its later days as a relief or duplicate vehicle at peak times. It stands next to West Riding **JHL 715**, a 1952 AEC Reliance/Roe, at Leeds. *(David Allen Collection)*

Above: Leaving Leeds for Castleford is **CHL 772** (**342**), a 1950 Daimler CVD6/Willowbrook 35-seat dual-purpose bus. It is appropriate that this bus has been preserved in running condition as it was the last bus to be registered by Bullocks, in May 1950. It left West Riding in 1967 first going to a Lancashire school. In 1972 it entered the preservation world and finally moved down to Somerset where it remains. *(David Allen Collection)*

Below: **CHL 746** (**340**), a 1950 Leyland Tiger PS2/Longford 33-seat coach, is seen in Wakefield outside the Savile Street depot in June 1960. It was withdrawn and scrapped in 1966. *(Roger Holmes)*

Above: A strange use for a 55-year-old bus. But all is not what it seems: **AHL 694 (284)** is a 1947 Barnaby-bodied Leyland Tiger PS1 and is one of only two known preserved Bullock buses. It came out of service in 1963 and eventually became a glider club mobile control room. Various attempts were then made to rebuild and preserve the vehicle without success. It was finally rebuilt into running condition in the North-East in 1993. In this photograph it is temporarily transformed for a part in television series. *(Malcolm King)*

Below: Two of the 1950 Seddon buses were converted to depot trucks in 1959. Here we see **CHL 742 (335)** at Wakefield in July 1965, a year before it was scrapped. *(Roger Holmes)*

Colour Section (2) - South Yorkshire

Above and below: When South Yorkshire was reformed in 1973, it moved out of the old-established Cornmarket base into premises in Northgate, Pontefract, which were refurbished for garage and office use. *(H-S Transport Collection)*

Above: **JWR 874 (71)**, a 1950 Albion CX 37/Strachan 55-seater, was one of three in that year - the final year South Yorkshire obtained vehicles from their traditional chassis manufacturer.

Below: **KWU 979 (74)**, a 1951 all-Leyland Titan PD2 55-seater, was one of four new that year. It is leaving Leeds for Pontefract. The batch was the first of many Leylands for South Yorkshire. *(Both: Malcolm King)*

Above and below: The first double-deck buses fitted with rear doors and concealed radiators (or tin fronts, as they were widely known), arrived in 1954/5. **OWR 264/5 (77/8)**, Leyland PD2 Titans with Bond 53-seat bodies, were photographed in Leeds. Bond was a Lancashire coachbuilder. The traditional style lettering used by the original company is clearly illustrated. *(Malcolm King)*

Above: The last halfcab buses came in 1960 with the new length 30ft bodies. **2600 WW (83)** represents the specification. It was a Leyland Titan PD3/Roe seating 63, and is seen in Pontefract sporting the new bold lettering of the 1973 reformed company. The high-backed seating favoured by South Yorkshire can also be seen. The bus remained in service until 1978.

Below: In 1963, the new generation rear-engined bus came into the fleet. **EWR 487C (87)** of the type dated from 1965. The Weymann-bodied Leyland Atlantean PDR1 is seen here on the long Leeds to Doncaster service. Maintaining the South Yorkshire semi-luxury standard, these vehicles were equipped with only 70 seats against the norm of 78. *(Both: Malcolm King)*

Above: As South Yorkshire changed direction in 1973, Daimler Fleetlines with Northern Counties bodywork became the standard double-deck bus, exemplified by **NWX 994M (94)** of 1973, one of a number purchased over the following few years *(David Allen Collection)*

Below: **DWX 397T (97)**, a 1978 Leyland Fleetline/Northern Counties, stands in Barnsley bus station. By this time, Daimler Fleetline production had moved north and was being marketed as a 'Leyland' product. *(Andrew Jarosz)*

Above: A number of Leyland Nationals were transferred from associated company West Riding into the South Yorkshire fleet. **EWX 213Y** (**113**) is pictured in Pontefract, newly painted, in 1996. *(H-S Transport Collection)*

Below: **CWR 506Y** (**506**), a 1982 Leyland Olympian/ECW, leaves Pontefract bus station in April 1995 on the Leeds to Doncaster service numbered by Metro as 411. This was one of the first buses to be transferred to the South Yorkshire fleet from West Riding after the Caldaire take-over. *(David Allen Collection)*

Above: Coaches came into the South Yorkshire fleet in some numbers when the company was reformed. The short-lived Manchester to Hull express service in particular required them. **YUG 820X (20)**, a 1982 Leyland Tiger/Plaxton, was one of four 53-seaters bought in the early 1980s; most had a service life of at least ten years with the company.

Below: Two more of the Tigers mentioned above are shown at the Northgate depot. **GNW 121/2Y (21/2)** dated from 1983. They were sold in 1995. *(Both: Andrew Jarosz)*

>> *Opposite page upper:* The first Leyland Olympians supplied to an independent operator arrived in 1982 and the model became South Yorkshire's standard double-decker. **A103 OUG (103)**, a 1984 example with Northern Counties bodywork with 71 semi-luxury seats, was photographed entering Pontefract bus station *en route* from Doncaster to Leeds. *(Malcolm King)*

Below: **C23 EUG (23)**, a Bova Futura 53-seat coach, arrived in 1986. It was withdrawn from use in 1994. *(David Allen Collection)*

Above: An assortment of buses was drafted into the South Yorkshire fleet from Caldaire/British Bus companies, mostly West Riding, which had a close operational link. Here is seen **SNS 824W** (**146**), a Leyland National 2 drafted in from elsewhere in the British Bus empire. *(David Allen Collection)*

Below: **G324 NNW** (**320**), a 1990 Leyland Lynx, is seen in Pontefract. This was another bus imported from the West Riding fleet to that of South Yorkshire. *(David Allen Collection)*

Above: **TWY 7** (**107/614**), a 1988 Leyland Olympian/Northern Counties, is seen parked in Central bus station, Leeds, displaying its new fleet number. It was the second generation bus to carry this cherished registration number, which first appeared on a 1957 South Yorkshire Leyland Titan PD2/Park Royal, No. 80.

Below: On a murky day in Pontefract, another South Yorkshire Olympian, 1990's **H106 RWT** (**106/615**), stands awaiting its departure time for Leeds. *(Both: Andrew Jarosz)*

Above: The final purchase made by South Yorkshire was of three Dennis Darts in January 1994. Being non-standard in the West Riding/Caldaire fleets, they were immediately passed to Yorkshire Traction. **L52 ONW (52)**, with its Plaxton Pointer 39-seat body, was photographed in the final days of operation. *(David Allen Collection)*

Below: On the demise of the Dennis Darts, Optare MetroRiders were drafted in from the West Riding fleet. **M749 WWR (749)**, dating from 1995, is seen at rest. *(Andrew Jarosz)*